INTRODUCING THE STAR OF THIS BOOK

TYRANNOSAURUS REX

(tie-RAN-

(x̄əɹ ss)

DID YOU KNOW...

that *T. rex* is one of the best killing machines ever to walk on Earth! Even though it wasn't the biggest carnivore that ever lived, it could have eaten pretty much anything it wanted and you'll soon find out why!

T. rex means 'tyrant lizard king'

D1514422

SETTING THE SCENE

· ·

It all started around 231 million years ago (mya), when the first dinosaurs appeared, part-way through the Triassic Period.

The Age of the Dinosaurs had begun, a time when dinosaurs would rule the world!

Scientists call this time the

MESOZOIC ERA
(mez-oh-zoh-ic)

and this era was so long that they divided it into three periods.

TRIASSIC
←······· lasted **51** million years ·······→

JURASSIC
←········· lasted **56** million years ·········

252 million years ago

201 million years ago

T. rex lived during the Cretaceous Period from 68 – 66 million years ago.

CRETACEOUS
←·········· lasted **79** million years ··········→

145 million years ago   **66** million years ago

WEATHER REPORT

The world didn't always look like it does today. Before the dinosaurs and during the early part of the Mesozoic Era the land was all stuck together in one supercontinent called Pangaea. Over time, things changed and by the end of the Cretaceous Period the land looked like this.

CRETACEOUS 66 mya

Name comes from the Latin word for 'chalk'

TRIASSIC

Very hot, dry and dusty

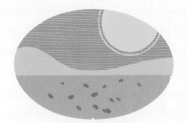

JURASSIC

Hot, humid and tropical

CRETACEOUS

Warm, wet and seasonal

During the Cretaceous Period the continents separated further and the world looked almost like it does today

HOMETOWN

Here's what's been discovered so far and where...

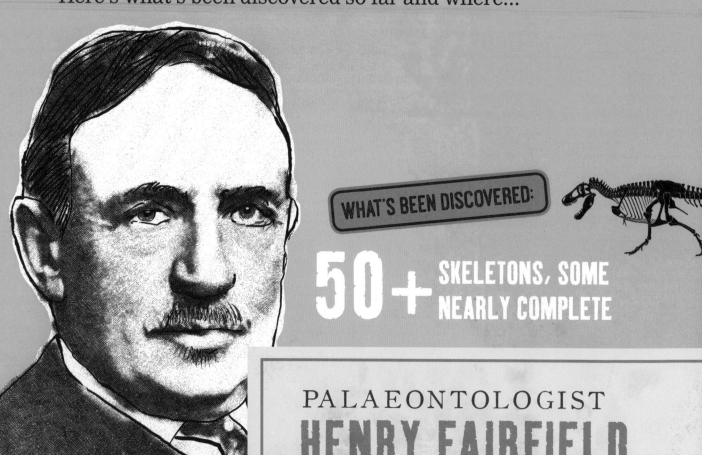

WHAT'S BEEN DISCOVERED:

50+ SKELETONS, SOME NEARLY COMPLETE

PALAEONTOLOGIST
HENRY FAIRFIELD OSBORN
NAMED TYRANNOSAURUS REX IN 1905

HELL CREEK, MONTANA

USA

LOTS OF SKULLS

EVEN T. REX POO HAS BEEN FOUND!

Found by Barnum Brown in Montana in 1902 on an expedition from the American Museum of Natural History, these first specimens amazed palaeontologists as *T. rex* was the first truly gigantic theropod (a group of dinosaurs that walked on two legs - bipedal) to be discovered.

Remains of *T. rex* have been discovered in many places across the USA and Canada. The most complete specimen was found in 1990 in South Dakota, nicknamed 'Sue'. Amazingly 90% of the skeleton was discovered!

VITAL STATISTICS

Some of the earliest dinosaurs were small and lightly built, the giants came later and *T. rex* was definitely one of those.

Let's look at *T. rex* and see what's special, quirky and downright amazing about this dinosaur!

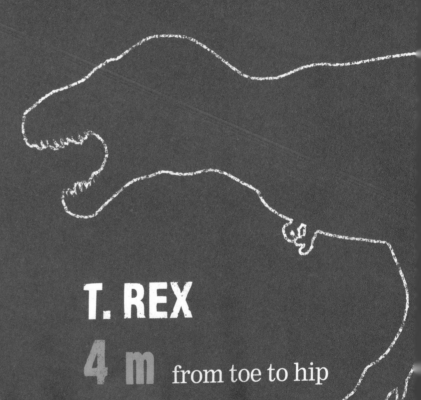

T. REX

4 m from toe to hip

T. rex was 4 m toe to hip, but up to 6 m high when rearing up and getting ready to attack, making it look even more scary!

hip height measurement

DOOR

2m high

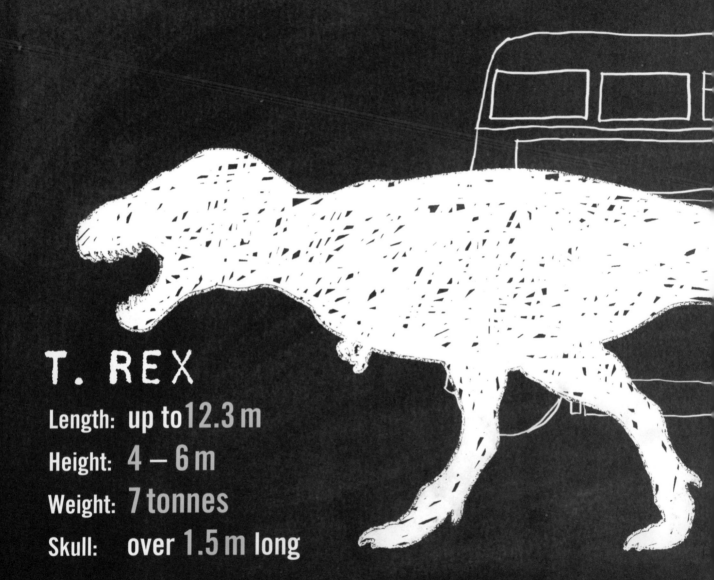

T. REX

Length: up to 12.3 m

Height: 4 – 6 m

Weight: 7 tonnes

Skull: over 1.5 m long

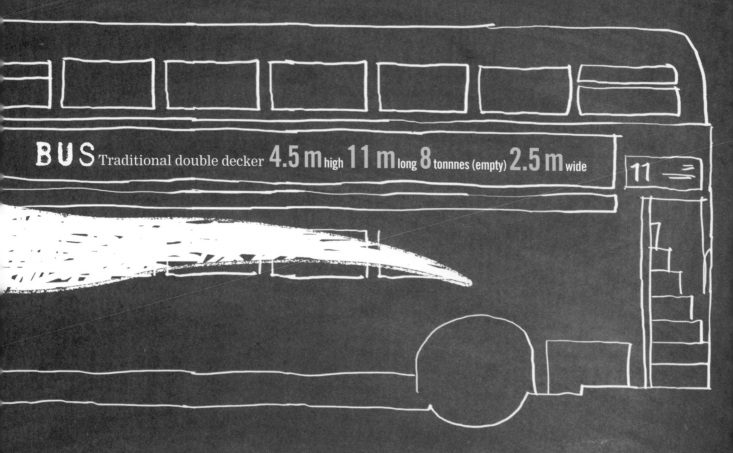

BUS Traditional double decker **4.5 m** high **11 m** long **8** tonnnes (empty) **2.5 m** wide   11

MOUSE

SCARY SCALE

How does *T. rex* rate?

NOT SCARY

| 1 | 2 | 3 | 4 | 5 |

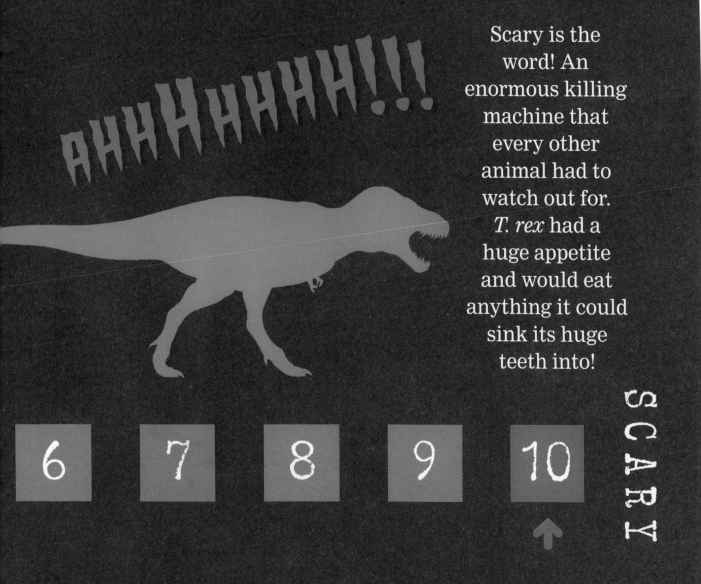

AHHHHHHHH!!!

Scary is the word! An enormous killing machine that every other animal had to watch out for. *T. rex* had a huge appetite and would eat anything it could sink its huge teeth into!

6 7 8 9 10

SCARY

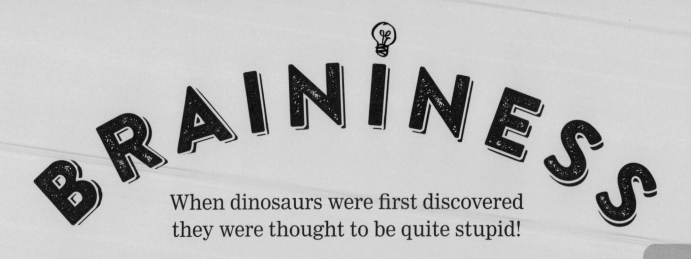

BRAININESS

When dinosaurs were first discovered
they were thought to be quite stupid!

Then a few scientists thought that some dinosaurs had
a second brain close to their butt! That's now just a myth.

Today scientists know that dinosaurs had one brain and were
intelligent for reptiles. Some were among the most intelligent
creatures alive during the Mesozoic Era, although
still not as smart as most modern mammals.

By looking at the:

Body size

Size
of the
brain

Sense
of
smell

Eyesight

Scientists can tell how they rated against each other...

WHERE DOES T. REX, A MEAT-EATING DINOSAUR, STAND ON THE 'BRAINY SCALE'?

TROODON
(TRU-oh-don)

$^{10}/10$
CARNIVORE

T. REX
(tie-RAN-oh-SAW-russ rex)

$^9/10$
CARNIVORE

ALLOSAURUS
(AL-oh-SAW-russ)

$^8/10$
CARNIVORE

IGUANODON
(ig-WAHN-oh-DON)

$^6/10$
HERBIVORE

STEGOSAURUS
(STEG-oh-SAW-russ)

$^4/10$
HERBIVORE

DIPLODOCUS
(DIP-lod-oh-CUSS)

$^2/10$
HERBIVORE

These dinosaurs are drawn to
scale in relation to each other!

SPEED-O-METER

SLOW

① ② ③ ④ ⑤

T. rex could reach up to 20 mph

T. rex had a solid body and strong legs with hollow bones so it was a powerful runner over short distances, but wouldn't have been able to keep up this speed for long as it was still very heavy at 7 tonnes!

6 7 8 9 10

FAST

WEAPONS

As one of the most efficient killing machines to ever walk the Earth, you won't be surprised to hear that *T. rex* had a lot of very special bits!

BITE

With a short muscly neck and a huge head that measured up to 1.5 m, *T. rex* had the most powerful bite of any land animal that has ever lived!

T. rex was capable of opening its mouth up to 80 º which is over 1 m wide, so *T. rex* could take huge mouthfuls.

T. *rex* had a great sense of smell, among the best of the meat-eating dinosaurs.

NOSE

More than one piece of preserved T. *rex* skin has been discovered, so scientists know that it was rough and scaly.

SKIN

EYES

T. *rex* had excellent vision. It had very large eyes, around 10 cm in diameter. The eyes were positioned on the side of its head, but faced forwards giving T. *rex* what is known as binocular vision where both eyes were used together, just like ours. It may even have been able to see well enough to hunt at night.

Scientists are confident that T. *rex* had feathers or fuzz-like protofeathers (early bird feathers) as one of its Chinese cousins certainly did, and were probably for insulation (keeping warm) and attracting a mate.

FEATHERS

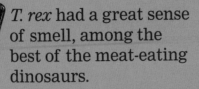

TEETH

With more than 50 strong, pointed banana-shaped teeth, they were designed to crush bone and tear flesh.

The largest was a whopping 30 cm long and this is a life-sized image of one of these massive teeth. Wow!

T. rex would bite, rip and swallow flesh and bone without chewing. The teeth, as with all dinosaurs, were constantly replaced, so if one tooth broke *T. rex* didn't have to worry as another would have grown in its place.

Tooth to scale!

DIET

MEAT, MEAT AND MORE MEAT!

Palaeontologists have discovered evidence of bite marks on some bones of both *Triceratops* and *Edmontosaurus*, which are thought to have been made by a *T. rex*!

WHO LIVED IN THE SAME NEIGHBOURHOOD?

Here are two dinosaurs that lived in the same woodlands as *T. rex*, which *T. rex* would have hunted...

EDMONTOSAURUS
(ed-MON-toe-SAW-russ)

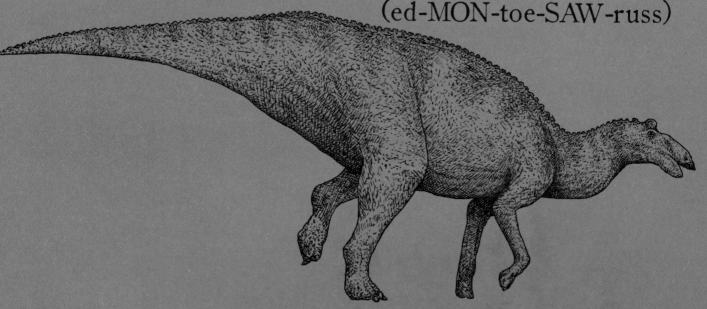

The first remains of *Edmontosaurus* were found in Edmonton, Canada, but other remains have been found across North America. It was a 9 m long, 3 tonne, plant-eating, duck-billed dinosaur with very few defences. This is why it is thought to have lived in herds - safety in numbers.

TRICERATOPS
(try-SAIR-uh-TOPS)

Many remains of *Triceratops* have been discovered across North America. At 8 m long, weighing in around 7 tonnes, and with its large set of brow horns and frill, it would have been an off-putting sight for a hungry *T. rex* but this didn't stop it trying!

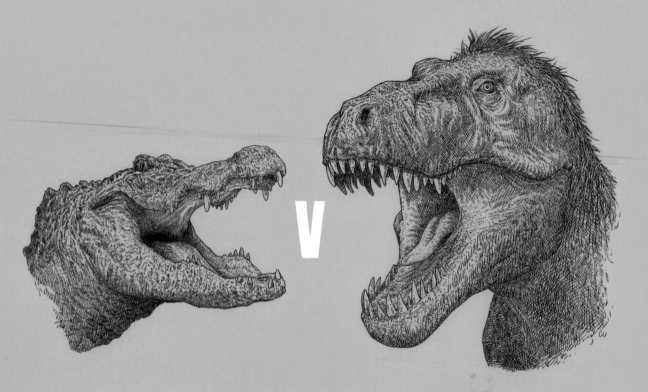

V

WHICH ANIMAL ALIVE TODAY IS MOST LIKE T. REX ?

As the apex (top) predator of its time, possibly the best killing machine that has ever walked on Earth, let's compare *T. rex* with an apex predator that is alive today.

ALLIGATOR V T. REX

	Alligator	T. Rex
LENGTH	up to 5.3 m	up to 12.3 m
WEIGHT	up to ½ tonne	up to 7 tonnes
DIET	carnivore	carnivore
WHERE	North America, Asia (China)	USA and Canada
TEETH	crunching not chewing, grew new teeth	crunching not chewing, grew new teeth
BITE	one of the most powerful today	most powerful of all land animals, EVER! 4 x more powerful than an alligator
TAIL	very important for swimming	very important for running
EYESIGHT	great, day & night	great in day & possibly at night
APPETITE	will eat anything	ditto!

WHAT'S SO SPECIAL ABOUT T. REX?

WHEN T. REX LIVED

CRETACEOUS 68 - 66 mya

TOOTH SIZE

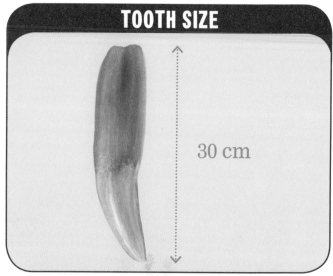

30 cm

WEIGHT

7 TONNES

FAST OR SLOW?

SPEED out of 10

7

THE BEST BITS!

DISCOVERED, SO FAR

50+ SKELETONS, SOME NEARLY COMPLETE

LOTS OF SKULLS

EVEN T. REX POO HAS BEEN FOUND!

HOW FRIGHTENING?

SCARY

10

MEAT OR PLANTS?

MEAT, MEAT AND MORE MEAT!

SPECIAL BITS

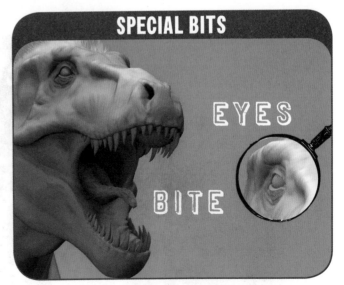

EYES

BITE

WHAT'S NEXT ?

OTHER EXCITING TITLES AVAILABLE NOW!

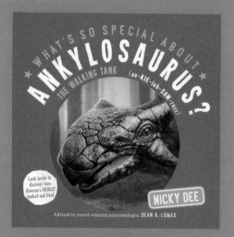

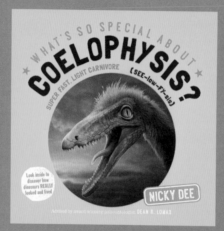

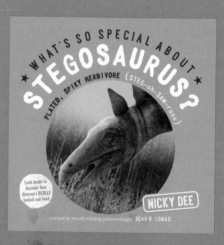

ANKYLOSAURUS
the walking tank

COELOPHYSIS
super-fast, light carnivore;
the first skull to travel
into space!

STEGOSAURUS
plated, spiky
herbivore

COMING SOON

Megalosaurus
the very first dinosaur
to be named

Triceratops
horned and frilled with
a massive skull

Diplodocus
long necked, whip-
tailed giant

Leaellynasaura
tiny, bug-eyed, long
tailed Australian